Brexit and Beyond: Navigating the UK's Political Landscape

In "Brexit and Beyond: Navigating the UK's Political Landscape," we embark on an insightful journey through the complex and ever-evolving world of British politics. This book provides a comprehensive exploration of the political landscape of the United Kingdom, with a particular focus on the tumultuous Brexit process and its profound impact on the nation. Beyond Brexit, we delve into the broader political themes and developments that continue to shape the UK's political landscape.

Table of Contents

Chapter 1: Understanding the UK Political System
- An overview of the UK's political institutions, including the Parliament, Monarchy, and Prime Minister's role.
- The historical context that led to the formation of the current political structure.

Chapter 2: The Road to Brexit
- The historical background of the European Union (EU) and the UK's relationship with it.

- The factors and events that led to the Brexit referendum in 2016.

Chapter 3: The Brexit Referendum
- An in-depth look at the referendum campaign, key arguments, and voter demographics.
- The outcome of the referendum and its immediate repercussions.

Chapter 4: Navigating the Brexit Process
- The complexities of negotiations, key players, and critical milestones during the Brexit process.
- The impact of Brexit on trade, immigration, and the UK's global position.

Chapter 5: Challenges and Opportunities Post-Brexit
- The challenges the UK faces as an independent nation.
- The opportunities for trade, diplomacy, and policy-making outside the EU.

Chapter 6: Political Parties and Alliances
- A review of major political parties in the UK, their ideologies, and positions on key issues.
- The dynamics of forming coalitions and alliances in British politics.

Chapter 7: Devolution and Regional Politics

- An examination of devolved governments in Scotland, Wales, and Northern Ireland.
- The role of regional politics in shaping national policies.

Chapter 8: Social and Cultural Dimensions
- The influence of social issues, demographics, and cultural factors on UK politics.
- The role of identity and multiculturalism in shaping political discourse.

Chapter 9: Political Activism and Civil Society
- The role of grassroots movements, protests, and civil society organizations in UK politics.
- How digital media and social networks are transforming political engagement.

Chapter 10: Future Challenges and Prospects
- An analysis of the potential challenges and opportunities that lie ahead for the UK.
- The impact of global trends, climate change, and technological advancements on UK politics.

Conclusion: Charting the Path Forward
- A reflection on the transformative journey the UK has undertaken, from Brexit to a post-EU era.
- The importance of active citizenship and informed political participation in shaping the nation's future.

"Brexit and Beyond: Navigating the UK's Political Landscape" provides a comprehensive and accessible guide to understanding the intricacies of British politics, offering readers a deeper insight into the country's past, present, and future. Whether you are a student, a political enthusiast, or simply interested in the political world, this book will equip you with the knowledge needed to navigate the fascinating world of UK politics in the 21st century.

Introduction:

In the wake of the historic Brexit referendum in 2016, the United Kingdom embarked on a journey that would not only redefine its relationship with the European Union but also reshape the very fabric of its political landscape. The decision to leave the EU sent shockwaves across the nation and around the world, sparking debates, divisions, and a profound sense of uncertainty about the future. Yet, Brexit was just one chapter in the intricate story of British politics, a story that extends far beyond its borders and encompasses a rich tapestry of history, culture, and governance.

"Brexit and Beyond: Navigating the UK's Political Landscape" is an exploration of this complex and multifaceted world, a journey that takes us through the corridors of power, the streets of activism, and the hearts and minds of a diverse and dynamic nation. In the following chapters, we will unravel the historical context that led to the formation of the United Kingdom's current political system and the pivotal moments that culminated in the Brexit referendum. We will navigate the intricacies of the Brexit process, dissecting negotiations, key players, and the myriad of challenges and opportunities it presented.

But this book goes beyond Brexit. It delves into the broader political themes and developments that continue to shape the UK's political landscape, from the role of political parties and alliances to the impact of devolution and regional politics. We will explore the influence of social and cultural factors, the dynamics of political activism and civil society, and the challenges and prospects that lie ahead for the UK in an increasingly interconnected and complex world.

Whether you are a student of politics, an engaged citizen, or simply curious about the political intricacies of the United Kingdom, this book offers a comprehensive and accessible guide to understanding the evolving nature of British politics in the 21st century. It is a journey through history, policy, and society, and an invitation to explore the diverse and dynamic world of the UK's political landscape. As we embark on this journey, we invite you to join us in unravelling the complexities, celebrating the achievements, and confronting the challenges of "Brexit and Beyond."

Chapter 1: Understanding the UK Political System

The United Kingdom's political landscape is a product of centuries of evolution, influenced by historical events, political reforms, and shifting societal values. To navigate the intricacies of British politics, we must first grasp the foundations of its political system. In this chapter, we will explore the fundamental elements that shape the UK's unique political structure.

1.1 The Historical Context

The roots of the UK's political system can be traced back through a rich and complex history. Key milestones include:

- Monarchy: For centuries, the UK was primarily governed by monarchs with varying degrees of power, from absolute rule to constitutional monarchy.

- Magna Carta (1215): A foundational document that limited the power of the monarchy and established certain legal principles that still influence the UK's legal system.

- Civil War and Glorious Revolution: These events in the 17th century led to the establishment of constitutional monarchy and parliamentary supremacy.

- Act of Union (1707 and 1801): The union of England, Scotland, and later Ireland into the United Kingdom created the modern political entity.

1.2 Key Political Institutions

The UK's political system revolves around several key institutions:

- Parliament: The UK Parliament is the supreme legislative body, consisting of two houses: the House of Commons (elected members) and the House of Lords (appointed members).

- Monarchy: The monarch holds a ceremonial role in government and performs various formal duties, such as opening Parliament and granting royal assent to legislation.

- Prime Minister: The Prime Minister is the head of government and the leader of the political party with the most seats in the House of Commons.

1.3 The Political Parties

The UK has a multi-party system, but two major parties dominate:

- Conservative Party: Traditionally associated with centre-right policies, the Conservatives have held government for much of the 20th and 21st centuries.

- Labour Party: Founded as a socialist party, Labour represents centre-left and progressive policies. It has also formed numerous governments.

- Liberal Democrats: A centrist party that often plays a pivotal role in coalition governments.

- Other Parties: Smaller parties like the Scottish National Party (SNP) and the Green Party have gained prominence, particularly in devolved regions.

1.4 Parliamentary Sovereignty

A cornerstone of the UK's political system is the principle of parliamentary sovereignty, which asserts that Parliament has the ultimate legal authority and can make or repeal any law. This concept, while providing a strong foundation for governance, has implications for the relationship between the UK and supranational bodies like the European Union.

1.5 Devolution

The UK's political landscape is not uniform across the entire nation. Devolution has granted varying degrees of self-governance to Scotland, Wales, and Northern Ireland, each with its own legislative body: the Scottish Parliament, Senedd (Welsh Parliament), and Northern Ireland Assembly, respectively. Devolution has allowed these regions to address local issues independently while remaining part of the United Kingdom.

1.6 Conclusion

Understanding the historical context, key institutions, political parties, and principles of the UK's political system is crucial as we embark on our journey through the intricacies of British politics. In the chapters that follow, we will delve deeper into the political dynamics, challenges, and opportunities that continue to shape the United Kingdom in the 21st century.

Chapter 2: The Road to Brexit

The decision for the United Kingdom to exit the European Union, commonly known as "Brexit," was a historic moment in British politics and had profound implications both domestically and internationally. In this chapter, we will explore the events, circumstances, and key milestones that led to the momentous Brexit referendum of 2016.

2.1 Historical Context

To understand Brexit, we must consider the UK's historical relationship with the European Union and its predecessors:

- The Common Market (EEC): The UK joined the European Economic Community (EEC), the precursor to the EU, in 1973, marking a significant shift in its international relations.

- The Maastricht Treaty (1992): This treaty expanded the scope of the EEC to include political and economic integration, paving the way for the EU's formation.

2.2 Euroscepticism in the UK

Euroscepticism, or the scepticism of EU membership, has been a persistent theme in UK politics. Key factors contributing to Euroscepticism include concerns about national sovereignty, immigration, and economic consequences.

2.3 The Role of Political Leaders

The positions of political leaders played a significant role in shaping public opinion:

- Margaret Thatcher: The former Prime Minister had a strained relationship with the EU and was sceptical of further integration.

- Tony Blair: Blair's Labour government was more pro-European, leading to closer ties with the EU.

2.4 The Global Financial Crisis

The global financial crisis of 2007-2008 had far-reaching economic consequences and contributed to a sense of economic insecurity in the UK, which played a role in the Brexit debate.

2.5 The Rise of UK Independence Party (UKIP)

UKIP, a political party advocating for British withdrawal from the EU, gained momentum in the early 21st century. Its electoral success and growing influence further fuelled the Brexit movement.

2.6 David Cameron's Pledge

To address internal divisions within the Conservative Party and to counter the UKIP threat, Prime Minister David Cameron pledged to hold a referendum on EU membership if the Conservatives won the 2015 general election. The promise was meant to be a demonstration of the government's commitment to democratic decision-making.

2.7 The Referendum Campaign

The official referendum campaign, which took place in 2016, was marked by passionate debates on both sides. Key arguments included issues related to immigration, trade, sovereignty, and the economic impact of Brexit.

2.8 The Outcome

On June 23, 2016, the UK held the Brexit referendum, in which 51.9% of voters chose to leave the European Union, while 48.1% voted to remain. The outcome sent shockwaves throughout the nation and the world.

2.9 Conclusion

The decision to hold the Brexit referendum and the outcome itself marked a turning point in the UK's political history. It revealed deep divisions within the country and initiated a complex and protracted process of disentangling the UK from the EU. The journey of Brexit and its multifaceted implications would dominate the political discourse in the UK for years to come, shaping the nation's future in ways that were yet to be fully realized. In the subsequent chapters, we will delve into the intricacies of the Brexit process and explore the challenges and opportunities it presented for the United Kingdom.

Chapter 3: The Brexit Referendum

The Brexit referendum of 2016 was a pivotal moment in British politics and had far-reaching consequences that continue to shape the United Kingdom's political landscape. In this chapter, we will delve into the details of the referendum campaign, the key arguments presented by both sides, and the immediate aftermath of the vote.

3.1 The Referendum Campaign

The official campaign period for the Brexit referendum was intense and passionate, with both the "Leave" and "Remain" camps vigorously advocating for their positions.

Leave Campaign

- Sovereignty: The Leave campaign argued that leaving the EU would restore the UK's sovereignty by ending the jurisdiction of the European Court of Justice and regaining control over its laws and regulations.

- Immigration: Concerns about immigration played a significant role, with the Leave camp arguing that leaving the EU would allow the UK to regain control over its borders and immigration policy.

- Trade Opportunities: Leave campaigners highlighted the potential for the UK to negotiate its own trade deals independently of EU agreements.

Remain Campaign

- Economic Stability: The Remain campaign emphasized the economic risks of leaving the EU, citing potential trade disruptions, reduced foreign investment, and job losses.

- Security and Influence: Remainers argued that EU membership enhanced the UK's security through intelligence sharing and its influence on global issues as part of a larger bloc.

- European Identity: Some argued that being part of the EU aligned with a broader European identity and that leaving would isolate the UK.

3.2 The Role of Media and Campaign Tactics

Media played a significant role in shaping public opinion during the campaign:

- Tabloid Newspapers: Some tabloid newspapers took a strong pro-Leave stance, while others supported Remain, influencing their readers' perspectives.

- Social Media: Social media platforms played a prominent role in the dissemination of campaign messages and mobilization of supporters.

- Campaign Tactics: Both sides employed various tactics, including rallies, televised debates, and door-to-door canvassing, to engage with voters.

3.3 The Outcome

On June 23, 2016, the UK voted in the Brexit referendum. The results were as follows:

- Leave: 51.9% of voters chose to leave the European Union.
- Remain: 48.1% of voters chose to remain in the EU.

The outcome was a narrow but clear victory for the Leave campaign. The result shocked many, and its implications began to unfold immediately.

3.4 Immediate Aftermath

- Resignation of David Cameron: Prime Minister David Cameron, who had campaigned for Remain, resigned in the wake of the referendum, leading to a leadership contest within the Conservative Party.

- Economic Uncertainty: Financial markets reacted with uncertainty, and the value of the British pound dropped significantly.

- Calls for Scottish Independence: The referendum result led to renewed calls for a second Scottish independence referendum, as Scotland had voted overwhelmingly to remain in the EU.

 3.5 Conclusion

The Brexit referendum marked a turning point in the UK's political history, with profound consequences that were only beginning to be understood. The decision to leave the EU initiated a complex and protracted process of negotiation, political realignment, and national introspection. The subsequent chapters will explore the intricate journey of Brexit, from negotiations with the EU to the challenges and opportunities it presented for the United Kingdom.

Chapter 4: Navigating the Brexit Process

With the referendum in the rear-view mirror and the decision to leave the European Union (EU) sealed, the United Kingdom embarked on a complex and challenging journey to extricate itself from the EU. In this chapter, we will explore the intricacies of the Brexit process, from the triggering of Article 50 to the finalization of the Withdrawal Agreement.

4.1 The Triggering of Article 50

The formal process of leaving the EU was initiated with the triggering of Article 50 of the Treaty on European Union:

- Article 50 Notification: On March 29, 2017, Prime Minister Theresa May officially triggered Article 50, beginning a two-year period of negotiations for the UK's withdrawal.

4.2 The Negotiating Teams

The Brexit negotiations involved key players on both sides:

- UK Negotiating Team: Led by various individuals, including David Davis, Dominic Raab, and Stephen Barclay, these teams represented the UK's interests.

- EU Negotiating Team: Chief EU negotiator Michel Barnier led the EU's negotiating efforts.

4.3 Key Issues in Negotiations

Several critical issues dominated the Brexit negotiations:

- Citizens' Rights: Ensuring the rights of EU citizens in the UK and UK citizens in the EU was a top priority.

- The "Divorce Bill": Negotiating the financial settlement to cover outstanding financial commitments to the EU.

- The Irish Border: Finding a solution to the complex issue of the border between Northern Ireland (part of the UK) and the Republic of Ireland (an EU member state).

4.4 The Withdrawal Agreement

After months of negotiations, a draft Withdrawal Agreement was reached:

- Backstop Arrangement: A contentious issue, the backstop was designed to prevent a hard border in Ireland if a future trade deal did not resolve the issue.

- UK Parliament Rejections: The agreement faced multiple rejections in the UK Parliament, leading to delays and further uncertainty.

4.5 Extensions and Delays

The UK's exit date from the EU was originally set for March 29, 2019. However, due to ongoing negotiations and political gridlock, the deadline was extended several times:

- First Extension: The UK received an extension until April 12, 2019.

- Second Extension: A further extension was granted until October 31, 2019.

4.6 Boris Johnson and the Revised Agreement

In July 2019, Boris Johnson became Prime Minister of the UK and renegotiated the Withdrawal Agreement:

- New Withdrawal Agreement: The revised agreement, which included changes to the backstop, was approved by the UK Parliament.

4.7 The End of EU Membership

The UK's EU membership officially ended on January 31, 2020:

- Transition Period: A transition period, during which the UK continued to follow EU rules and regulations, lasted until December 31, 2020.

4.8 Conclusion

The Brexit process was a long and arduous journey, marked by political turmoil, negotiations, and significant legal and logistical challenges. With the UK formally exiting the EU, attention turned to the future relationship between the two entities, including trade agreements, security cooperation, and broader diplomatic ties. In the subsequent chapters, we will delve into the challenges and opportunities that Brexit presented for the United Kingdom on both domestic and international fronts.

Chapter 5: Challenges and Opportunities Post-Brexit

With the United Kingdom formally exiting the European Union (EU), a new chapter in its history began. This chapter explores the multifaceted challenges and opportunities that emerged in the post-Brexit era, both domestically and on the international stage.

5.1 Economic Realities

The UK's departure from the EU had immediate economic implications:

- Trade Disruptions: Businesses faced new customs checks and trade barriers with the EU, leading to disruptions in supply chains and increased costs.

- Currency Volatility: The value of the British pound fluctuated, affecting exchange rates and international trade.

- Economic Impact: The COVID-19 pandemic, which coincided with Brexit, added further economic challenges.

5.2 Trade Agreements

One of the central post-Brexit objectives was to negotiate new trade agreements:

- EU-UK Trade and Cooperation Agreement: This agreement, reached in December 2020, outlined the future trading relationship between the UK and the EU.

- Other Trade Agreements: The UK sought to negotiate trade deals with other countries, including the United States, Japan, and Australia.

5.3 Northern Ireland Protocol

The Northern Ireland Protocol was designed to prevent a hard border between Northern Ireland (part of the UK) and the Republic of Ireland (an EU member state):

- Trade Barriers: The protocol led to new customs checks and regulations on goods moving between Great Britain and Northern Ireland.

- Controversy: It became a contentious issue in UK politics, with some viewing it as a barrier to internal UK trade.

5.4 Immigration and Borders

The UK implemented a new points-based immigration system:

- Skill-Based Immigration: The system prioritizes skilled workers and seeks to control immigration numbers.

- Impact on Industries: Some sectors, such as agriculture and healthcare, faced labour shortages.

5.5 Sovereignty and Independence

Brexit was framed by some as an assertion of national sovereignty:

- Regulatory Autonomy: The UK regained the ability to set its own regulations and standards.

- International Relations: The UK pursued an independent foreign policy and expanded its global presence.

5.6 Challenges for Scotland and Wales

The devolved governments in Scotland and Wales had different perspectives on Brexit:

- Scottish Independence: Brexit reignited calls for Scottish independence, with many Scots wishing to remain in the EU.

- Welsh Concerns: Wales, while predominantly pro-Brexit, had concerns about the economic impact.

5.7 Global Britain

The concept of "Global Britain" emerged as a vision for the UK's role in the world:

- International Alliances: The UK sought to strengthen ties with Commonwealth nations and expand its global influence.

- Foreign Aid and Diplomacy: The government emphasized humanitarian efforts and international diplomacy.

5.8 Conclusion

The post-Brexit landscape presented the United Kingdom with a complex set of challenges and opportunities. The nation grappled with economic disruptions, trade negotiations, and questions of sovereignty, while also charting a new course on the global stage. As the UK continued to navigate this uncharted territory, its decisions and actions would have enduring consequences, shaping its future role in the international community and its domestic policies for years to come. In the subsequent chapters, we will delve deeper into the social and political dimensions of post-Brexit Britain.

Chapter 6: Political Parties and Alliances

The political landscape of the United Kingdom has undergone significant changes in the wake of Brexit and the evolving challenges and opportunities it has presented. In this chapter, we explore the role of political parties and alliances in shaping post-Brexit British politics.

6.1 The Conservative Party

The Conservative Party, traditionally associated with centre-right policies, played a central role in driving the Brexit process:

- Leadership Change: Boris Johnson's leadership of the Conservative Party and the government brought a renewed focus on delivering Brexit.

- Red Wall Gains: In the 2019 general election, the Conservatives made significant gains in traditionally Labour-held constituencies in northern England, known as the "Red Wall."

- Brexit as a Unifying Issue: The party's stance on Brexit helped consolidate its support base and secure a majority in the House of Commons.

6.2 The Labour Party

The Labour Party, traditionally centre-left and progressive, faced internal divisions over Brexit:

- Leadership Changes: Jeremy Corbyn's leadership was marked by ambiguity on Brexit, leading to criticism within the party.

- Election Defeat: The Labour Party experienced a significant defeat in the 2019 general election, prompting a leadership change and a reassessment of its policies and messaging.

6.3 Other Political Parties

Smaller parties also played roles in post-Brexit politics:

- Liberal Democrats: The Liberal Democrats, with a pro-Remain stance, sought to rebuild their support base.

- Scottish National Party (SNP): The SNP, advocating for Scottish independence and EU membership, continued to exert influence in Scotland.

- Green Party: The Green Party focused on environmental and social justice issues.

6.4 Brexit Party and Reform UK

The Brexit Party, led by Nigel Farage, played a key role in advocating for Brexit:

- European Parliament Elections: In the 2019 European Parliament elections, the Brexit Party emerged as the largest UK party, reflecting the strong pro-Brexit sentiment.

- Reform UK: The Brexit Party later rebranded as Reform UK, emphasizing broader political reform beyond Brexit.

6.5 Coalition Building and Alliances

The complexities of post-Brexit politics led to discussions of potential coalitions and alliances:

- Northern Ireland: The Democratic Unionist Party (DUP) and Sinn Féin remained key players in Northern Ireland's political landscape.

- Wales: Plaid Cymru, the party advocating for Welsh independence, continued to seek influence in Welsh politics.

- Scottish Independence: The issue of Scottish independence remained prominent, with debates about a potential second independence referendum.

6.6 Conclusion

The post-Brexit political landscape in the United Kingdom has been marked by realignments, shifting voter priorities, and evolving party dynamics. As the nation grapples with the challenges and opportunities of life outside the EU, political parties and alliances continue to adapt to a new era of British politics. The outcomes of future elections and the direction of policy decisions will shape the trajectory of the UK's political journey in the years to come. In the subsequent chapters, we will explore the implications of these political changes on broader societal and regional issues.

Chapter 7: Devolution and Regional Politics

Devolution, the delegation of certain powers to regional governments within the United Kingdom, has played a significant role in shaping the nation's political landscape. In this chapter, we examine the impact of devolution and the dynamics of regional politics in a post-Brexit era.

7.1 Devolved Governments

The UK has three devolved governments, each with varying degrees of legislative power:

- Scottish Parliament: Established in 1999, the Scottish Parliament has authority over areas such as education, healthcare, and justice.

- Senedd (Welsh Parliament): The Senedd, created in 1999, has powers over areas including health, education, and transport.

- Northern Ireland Assembly: After periods of suspension, the Northern Ireland Assembly was restored in 2020, overseeing issues like healthcare, education, and justice.

7.2 The Impact of Brexit

Devolution has been deeply impacted by Brexit:

- Differing Stances: Scotland and Northern Ireland voted to remain in the EU, while Wales voted to leave. These differing positions created tensions within the UK.

- Devolved Consent: Questions arose about the consent of devolved governments for UK-wide policies, particularly in areas affected by EU laws.

7.3 Scottish Independence

The issue of Scottish independence remains a central concern:

- Second Independence Referendum: The Scottish National Party (SNP) continued to push for a second independence referendum, arguing that the changed circumstances of Brexit justified a new vote.

- Debate and Division: The debate over Scottish independence has been marked by passionate arguments on both sides, with questions about the economic, political, and social implications.

7.4 Welsh Devolution

Wales, while predominantly pro-Brexit, has its own devolved government:

- Growing Autonomy: Calls for increased powers for the Senedd have grown, with discussions about potential future referendums on Welsh independence.

- Regional Variations: The Welsh government has adopted different policies in some areas, such as education, leading to regional variations in governance.

7.5 Northern Ireland and Brexit

Brexit posed unique challenges for Northern Ireland:

- The Northern Ireland Protocol: To avoid a hard border with the Republic of Ireland, Northern Ireland remained aligned with some EU rules, leading to new customs checks with Great Britain.

- Political Implications: The Protocol became a source of political tension and contributed to discussions about the potential reunification of Ireland.

7.6 The Role of Regional Parties

Regional parties have played influential roles in devolved governments:

- SNP in Scotland: The SNP has governed Scotland and advocated for independence, shaping Scottish politics.

- Sinn Féin in Northern Ireland: Sinn Féin became a prominent voice in Northern Ireland politics and pushed for reunification.

- Plaid Cymru in Wales: Plaid Cymru has continued to advocate for Welsh independence and has influenced policy discussions.

7.7 Conclusion

Devolution and regional politics have added complexity to the United Kingdom's political landscape, especially in the context of Brexit and debates over sovereignty. The future direction of devolution, the potential for referendums, and the balance of power between devolved governments and Westminster will continue to be critical issues in the post-Brexit era. In the subsequent chapters, we will delve into social and cultural dimensions, as well as the role of activism and civil society in post-Brexit Britain.

Chapter 8: Social and Cultural Dimensions

The social and cultural dimensions of post-Brexit Britain are deeply intertwined with the political landscape. In this chapter, we explore how Brexit has influenced identity, multiculturalism, and societal values within the United Kingdom.

8.1 Identity and Nationalism

Brexit has sparked discussions about identity and nationalism:

- British Identity: Some saw Brexit as a reassertion of British identity and sovereignty, emphasizing historical ties and cultural heritage.

- Scottish and Welsh Identity: In Scotland and Wales, debates about independence have also revolved around national identity and distinct cultural identities.

8.2 Multiculturalism and Immigration

Brexit's impact on immigration and multiculturalism has been a significant aspect of post-Brexit Britain:

- Immigration Policy: The UK introduced a points-based immigration system, aiming to attract skilled workers while controlling immigration numbers.

- National Conversations: Brexit prompted discussions about the role of immigration, diversity, and integration in British society.

8.3 Regional Disparities

Regional disparities in economic opportunities and development have been highlighted:

- Economic Divisions: Brexit exposed economic inequalities between regions, contributing to debates about government investment and support.

-	Redistribution: Discussions about redistributing resources to address regional imbalances have gained traction.

8.4 Cultural Exchange and Education

Brexit has implications for cultural exchange and education:

- Student Mobility: Changes in immigration policies and funding have affected the mobility of students and researchers.

- Arts and Culture: The cultural and creative industries have explored new opportunities for international collaboration and partnerships.

8.5 Environmental and Climate Concerns

Environmental issues have become more prominent in the wake of Brexit:

- Environmental Regulations: Questions have arisen about the alignment of UK environmental regulations with EU standards.

- Climate Policies: The UK has set ambitious climate targets, leading to discussions about environmental policy and sustainability.

8.6 Social Activism and Civil Society

Brexit has energized social activism and civil society engagement:

- Protests and Demonstrations: Activists have organized protests and campaigns on various issues, including climate change and social justice.

- Community Initiatives: Grassroots movements and community-based initiatives have thrived.

8.7 Conclusion

Brexit has cast a spotlight on the social and cultural dynamics that shape the United Kingdom. Debates about identity, immigration, and regional disparities continue to evolve, reflecting the complex and multifaceted nature of British society. As the UK charts its course in a post-Brexit world, addressing these social and cultural dimensions will be essential for shaping a cohesive and inclusive future. In the subsequent chapters, we will delve into the role of political activism and civil society in post-

Brexit Britain, as well as the challenges and prospects on the global stage.

Chapter 9: Political Activism and Civil Society

In the aftermath of Brexit, political activism and civil society organizations have played pivotal roles in shaping public discourse, advocating for various causes, and holding political leaders accountable. This chapter explores the impact of activism and the evolving role of civil society in post-Brexit Britain.

9.1 Grassroots Movements

Brexit galvanized a range of grassroots movements and campaigns:

- Pro-European Movements: Groups advocating for a closer relationship with the EU, a second referendum, or the reversal of Brexit gained prominence.

- Youth Activism: Young activists organized protests, engaged in voter registration drives, and voiced concerns about their futures in a post-Brexit world.

9.2 Protests and Demonstrations

Protests and demonstrations have been a visible expression of political activism:

- Anti-Brexit Protests: Large-scale protests in cities like London drew attention to the passionate opposition to Brexit.

- Environmental Protests: Climate change activists, including Extinction Rebellion, used civil disobedience to push for action on environmental issues.

9.3 Social Justice Campaigns

Activism extended to social justice causes:

- Black Lives Matter: The global movement gained momentum in the UK, sparking discussions about systemic racism and police reform.

- Gender Equality: Advocates continued to push for gender equality and combat gender-based violence.

9.4 Online Activism and Digital Campaigning

Social media and digital platforms have been instrumental in organizing and amplifying activist efforts:

- Online Petitions: Campaigns and petitions on platforms like Change.org and Parliament's website garnered millions of signatures on various issues.

- Social Media Campaigns: Hashtag movements and viral campaigns facilitated awareness and engagement.

9.5 Civil Society Organizations

Civil society organizations have played a crucial role in post-Brexit Britain:

- Think Tanks: Policy research institutions have contributed analysis and recommendations on Brexit-related issues.

- Advocacy Groups: Organizations focused on specific causes, such as human rights, immigration, and healthcare, have lobbied for policy changes.

9.6 Challenges and Opportunities

While activism and civil society engagement have been influential, they have also faced challenges:

- Polarization: Brexit and related issues have polarized public opinion, making consensus-building more challenging.

- Funding: Some organizations have faced financial constraints, impacting their ability to advocate effectively.

9.7 Conclusion

Political activism and civil society have been vibrant and dynamic forces in the post-Brexit landscape of the United Kingdom. They have shaped public opinion, influenced policy debates, and served as checks and balances on political power. As the nation navigates the complexities of its post-EU future, the role of activism and civil society will continue to evolve, presenting both challenges and opportunities for democratic engagement and societal change. In the final chapter, we will explore the United Kingdom's role on the global stage and the challenges and prospects it faces in a rapidly changing world.

Chapter 10: The United Kingdom on the Global Stage

The United Kingdom's departure from the European Union marked a significant shift in its international relations and global positioning. In this final chapter, we examine the UK's role on the global stage, its diplomatic endeavours, and the challenges and prospects it faces in a rapidly changing world.

10.1 Global Diplomacy

Post-Brexit, the UK has sought to redefine its diplomatic relationships:

- "Global Britain": The concept of "Global Britain" has been central to the UK's vision for an independent foreign policy.

- Trade Agreements: The UK has pursued trade agreements with countries beyond the EU, including the United States, Japan, and Australia.

10.2 Relations with the European Union

The UK's relationship with the EU remains a critical aspect of its foreign policy:

- The EU-UK Trade and Cooperation Agreement: This agreement outlines the future trading relationship and cooperation in various areas, including security and law enforcement.

- Ongoing Negotiations: Ongoing discussions with the EU on issues such as financial services and data sharing continue to shape the relationship.

10.3 Multilateral Organizations

The UK has reaffirmed its commitment to multilateral organizations and international institutions:

- United Nations: The UK remains a member of the United Nations and has taken on leadership roles in areas like climate action.

- NATO: The UK continues to be a key member of NATO, contributing to international security.

10.4 Humanitarian Efforts

The UK has emphasized humanitarian efforts and development aid:

- Foreign Aid: Despite debates about foreign aid spending, the UK has maintained its commitment to international development.

- Global Health Initiatives: The UK has played a role in global health initiatives, including responses to pandemics.

 10.5 Climate Leadership

The UK has set ambitious climate goals and hosted international climate conferences:

- COP26: The UK hosted the 26th UN Climate Change Conference of the Parties (COP26) in Glasgow, where global leaders discussed climate action.

- Net Zero Commitment: The UK has committed to achieving net-zero carbon emissions by 2050.

 10.6 Challenges and Prospects

The UK's global role faces challenges and prospects:

- Economic Impact: The economic consequences of Brexit and the COVID-19 pandemic have shaped the UK's global engagement.

- Global Realignment: The UK must navigate evolving global power dynamics and changing alliances.

 10.7 Conclusion

As the United Kingdom charts its path on the global stage in a post-Brexit era, it faces a complex array of challenges and opportunities. Its role in trade, diplomacy, climate leadership, and international development will continue to evolve, shaping its identity and influence in a rapidly changing world. The future will depend on the nation's ability to adapt to global challenges, forge new alliances, and leverage its strengths to make a positive impact on the international stage.

Conclusion: Navigating the Post-Brexit Landscape

The story of post-Brexit Britain is one of transformation, complexity, and resilience. The decision to leave the European Union set the

United Kingdom on a course that reshaped its political, economic, and social landscape in profound ways. As we conclude this exploration of post-Brexit Britain, the nation faces a future filled with both challenges and opportunities.

Brexit was not merely an event but a catalyst for change, prompting discussions about sovereignty, identity, and the nation's place in the world. It revealed deep divisions within society, reflected in political debates, regional disparities, and contrasting visions for the country's future. At the same time, it unleashed energies of activism and civil society engagement, underscoring the importance of democratic participation and the power of collective voices.

Economically, the United Kingdom faced disruptions and uncertainties as it adjusted to new trade arrangements and navigated the economic impact of the COVID-19 pandemic. Trade negotiations, regulatory autonomy, and economic realignments became defining features of post-Brexit economic realities.

On the global stage, the UK embarked on a journey to redefine its international relations and diplomatic endeavours. The concept of "Global Britain" signalled its aspiration to play a prominent role in global affairs, from trade agreements to climate leadership and humanitarian efforts. It remained a key player in multilateral organizations while navigating its evolving relationship with the European Union.

In terms of domestic politics, Brexit reshaped political parties, realigned voter priorities, and fuelled discussions about the future of devolution and regional politics. The question of Scottish independence, the role of regional parties, and debates over national identity continue to shape political discourse.

The social and cultural dimensions of post-Brexit Britain were marked by discussions about identity, multiculturalism, and societal values. Immigration, regional disparities, and environmental concerns became central topics in public discourse, reflecting a nation grappling with the complexities of its changing identity.

Amidst these challenges, political activism and civil society organizations emerged as vibrant forces, energized by passionate advocates seeking to shape the future of their nation. Protests, grassroots movements, and social justice campaigns underscored the importance of civic engagement and the power of collective action.

As the United Kingdom moves forward in the post-Brexit era, it faces the task of addressing these challenges while embracing the opportunities that come with newfound autonomy and global presence. The ability to forge consensus, bridge divisions, and leverage its strengths will be essential in shaping a cohesive and prosperous future.

Brexit was a turning point in the nation's history, but it is not the end of the story. The United Kingdom's journey continues, with its people, institutions, and leaders shaping the path ahead. In the dynamic and ever-evolving landscape of post-Brexit Britain, one thing remains certain: the resilience and adaptability of a nation that has always faced challenges with determination and resolve.

Bibliography

Books

1. Clarke, Harold D., Goodwin, Matthew, and Whiteley, Paul. (2017). "Brexit: Why Britain Voted to Leave the European Union."

2. Shipman, Tim. (2017). "Brexit: The Uncivil War."

3. Cleppe, Pieter. (2020). "Post-Brexit UK-EU Trade Relations: A Comprehensive Guide."

4. Evans, Geoffrey and Menon, Anand (Eds.). (2017). "Brexit and British Politics."

5. Green, David Allen. (2020). "Brexit: A Very Short Introduction."

Websites

1. [UK Government Brexit Website](https://www.gov.uk/brexit)

2. [European Union Brexit Website](https://ec.europa.eu/info/brexit/brexit-preparedness_en)

3. [The Institute for Government](https://www.instituteforgovernment.org.uk/brexit)

4. [The Guardian - Brexit Section](https://www.theguardian.com/politics/eu-referendum)

Academic Journals

1. "Brexit and Public Opinion" - Published in "Political Insight."

2. "Brexit and the Political Economy of UK Trade: A Comprehensive Review of the Academic Literature" - Published in "World Trade Review."

Multimedia

1. [BBC Brexit Explained](https://www.bbc.co.uk/news/politics/uk_leaves_the_eu)

2. [Brexit: The Movie](https://www.youtube.com/watch?v=UTMxfAkxfQ0)

3. [Brexitcast Podcast](https://www.bbc.co.uk/programmes/p05299nl)

These resources encompass a wide range of sources, including books, websites, academic journals, and multimedia materials, offering a comprehensive view of the topic of Brexit and its impact on the United Kingdom.